NEVER ASK A MAN

THE SIZE

OF HIS SPREAD

GLADIOLA MONTANA

NEVER ASK A MAN

THE SIZE

OF HIS SPREAD

A COWGIRL'S
GUIDE TO LIFE

GIBBS SMITH
TO ENRICH AND INSPIRE HUMANKIND
Salt Lake City | Charleston | Santa Fe | Santa Barbara

Revised Edition
13 12   20 19 18 17 16 15 14 13 12 11 10 9 8 7

Text copyright © 1993 by Gibbs Smith, Publisher
The quotations in this book come from a mixture
of lore and experience.
Animation by Richard Haight, © 1993 Gibbs Smith, Publisher

Published by
Gibbs Smith
P.O. Box 667
Layton, UT 84041

Orders: 1.800.835.4993
www.gibbs-smith.com

Design by Black Eye Design
Printed and bound in the U. S. A.
Gibbs Smith books are printed on either recycled, 100 percent post-
consumer waste, FSC-certified papers or on paper produced from a
100 percent certified sustainable forest-controlled wood source.

The Library of Congress has cataloged the earlier edition as follows:

Montana, Gladiola
   Never ask a man the size of his spread : a cowgirl's guide to life /
Gladiola Montana.
      p. cm.
ISBN 13: 978-0-87905-554-7 (first edition)
ISBN 10: 0-87905-554-5 (first edition)
   1. Cowgirls-West (U.S.)—Humor. I. Title.
F596.M655   1993
978-dc20

                                           92-43920

ISBN 13: 978-1-4236-0705-2
ISBN 10: 1-4236-0705-8

THE CODE OF HER WEST

Use a short rope, a sweet smile, and a hot brand.

CALLIN' WOMEN
the weaker sex makes
about as much sense

as callin' men the stronger one.

WHETHER A HORSE
turns out to be a good
cow horse or a poor one
pretty much depends on the
intelligence of the handler.

When a cowboy
gives you the key
to his truck,
you know
you're close to
winning the key
to his heart.

Anybody
who thinks
they know
everything
ain't been
around
long enough
to know
ANYTHING.

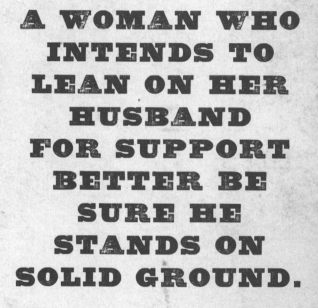

A WOMAN WHO
INTENDS TO
LEAN ON HER
HUSBAND
FOR SUPPORT
BETTER BE
SURE HE
STANDS ON
SOLID GROUND.

Foolin' a man
ain't all
that hard.

Finding one
that ain't a fool
is a lot harder.

IF YOU DON'T GET MARRIED
you'll never have a good man.

★★★

On the other hand,
if you ain't married
you don't need one.

SOME
THINGS
DON'T NEED
ALL THE
THOUGHT
PEOPLE
GIVE 'EM.

OIL ALL THE
WHEELS ON
YOUR WAGON,
NOT JUST THE
SQUEAKY ONE.

Learn to tie some USEFUL knots.

The time to
dance is when
the music's
playin'.

"ONE OF THESE DAYS" IS "NONE OF THESE DAYS."

If a horse makes a few
good moves on his own,
HE SHOULD BE REWARDED
so that he will develop others.

If you're havin'
trouble with
a mustang,
change the bit.

You can't
GET AHEAD
of anybody
you're tryin'
to get even
with.

THERE'S NO NEED TO
buckle on chaps and spurs
just to drive the milk cows in.

IF YOU WAKE
UP AND FIND
YOURSELF A
SUCCESS, YOU
AIN'T BEEN
ASLEEP.

HIGH
STEPPERS
GIVE
BUMPY
RIDES.

When somebody commences
to flatterin' you, there's
generally more up their sleeve
THAN JUST AN ARM.

You don't have to wait for someone to bring you flowers— PLANT YOUR OWN GARDEN.

BE SURE
TO TASTE
YOUR WORDS
BEFORE YOU
SPIT 'EM OUT.

You can't
keep trouble
from visitin',
✦✦
but you
don't have
to offer it
A CHAIR.

Women have a
lot of courage;
otherwise, none
would ever get
married.

IT'S PRUDENT TO SPEND less time tryin' to figure out who's right and more time tryin' to figure out what's right.

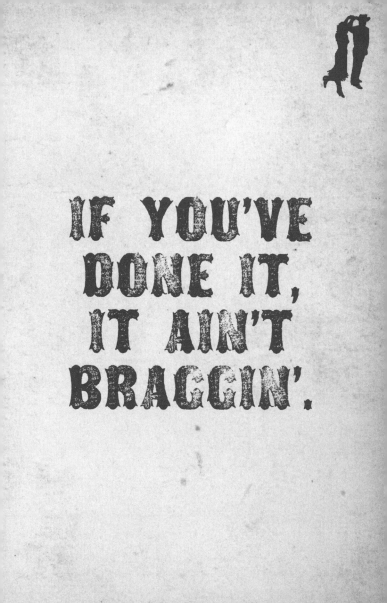

IF YOU'VE DONE IT, IT AIN'T BRAGGIN'.

RUNNIN' FROM PROBLEMS IS A SURE WAY OF RUNNIN' INTO PROBLEMS.

You can't drown your sorrows;

★ ★ ★

they know how to SWIM.

If you find
some happiness
inside yourself,
you'll start
findin' it in
a lot of other
places too.

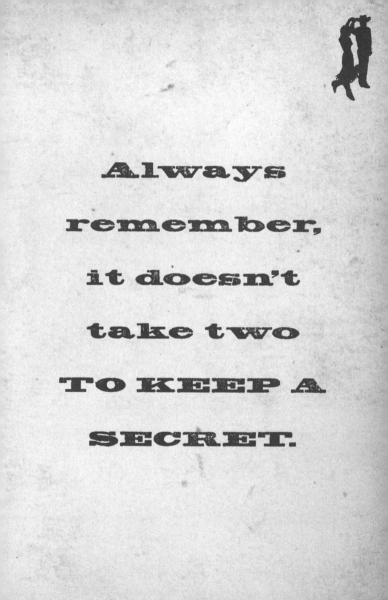

Always remember, it doesn't take two TO KEEP A SECRET.

A HABIT IS EITHER A BLESSING OR A CURSE.

✴ ✴

THINK ABOUT THAT WHEN YOU FIND YOU'VE FALLEN INTO ONE.

If you want a little EXTRA
ATTENTION, ask your
husband if you can borrow
his six-shooter for the night.

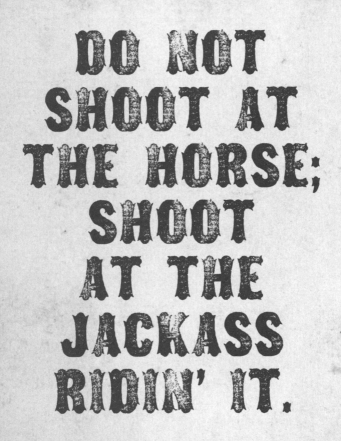

DO NOT SHOOT AT THE HORSE; SHOOT AT THE JACKASS RIDIN' IT.

When you get wind of a tail,
you're following **TOO CLOSE**.

SHEEP DON'T
ASSOCIATE
WITH WOLVES
—AND FOR A
DANG GOOD
REASON.

Cryin' about
a bad past is
a WASTE of
good tears.

Always try to
MAKE FOLKS HAPPY,

even if that means going out
of your way to avoid 'em.

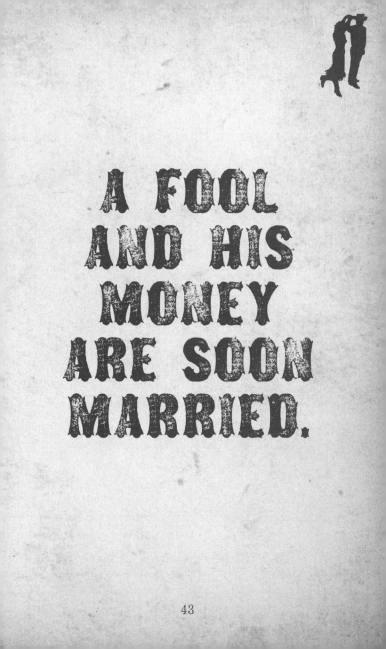

A FOOL
AND HIS
MONEY
ARE SOON
MARRIED.

If you don't have a good reason to do something, then you've got a dang good reason not to do it.

When you see a turtle sittin'
on a fence post, you may
not know how it got there,
but you can be darn sure
IT HAD HELP.

If you
wanta
SAY NO,

it's best
to say it
right away.

DON'T BURN DOWN YOUR HOUSE TO KILL A RAT.

A woman's intuition comes from payin' attention to what's goin' on around her.

THERE ARE TWO KINDS
of people in this ol' world;
those who believe there are
two kinds of people, and
those who know better.

NEW AND IMPROVED CAN'T BEAT TRIED AND TRUE.

When kissin' a cowboy
in the rain,
make sure you both fit
UNDER HIS HAT.

A LOT OF FAMILIES
headed west with no more
than bedding, buckets, Bibles,
and high hopes. That's a
pretty good start.

YOU'LL MAKE
BETTER
PROGRESS
IF YOU GET
OUT OF YOUR
OWN WAY.

Be wary of

puppy love;

✦✦

it can

lead to a

DOG'S LIFE.

A LESSON EVERY COWGIRL
should learn is where
her business ends and
someone else's starts.

**Never—
under any
circumstances—
admit that you
like to cook.**

PEOPLE WHOSE MANNERS
are on the absent side are
probably missin' more than
just their manners.

You can warm your socks in the oven,

but that DON'T make 'em BISCUITS.

YOU HAVE TO
TAKE RANCH
COUNTRY FOR
WHAT IT IS,
NOT WHAT IT
OUGHT TO BE.

BRAND WHAT NEEDS TO BE BRANDED.

A lot of things that don't look
GOOD IN THEIR RAW FORM
turn out to be pretty good
when they're finished.

Share your
WISDOM,
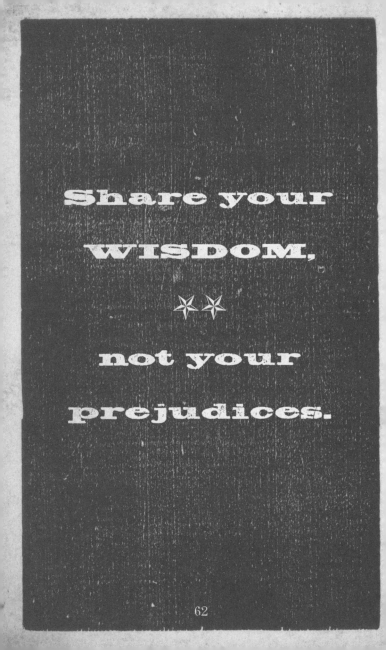
not your
prejudices.

Not all fillies ride well the first time out.

DON'T HANG YOUR HAT ON SOMEONE ELSE'S PEG.

There are many
kinds of bandits

★ ★ ★

so sit on your wallet and
hold onto your heart.

It's not what
you say
to a horse
that gets its
attention.

✴✴

It's how you
say it.

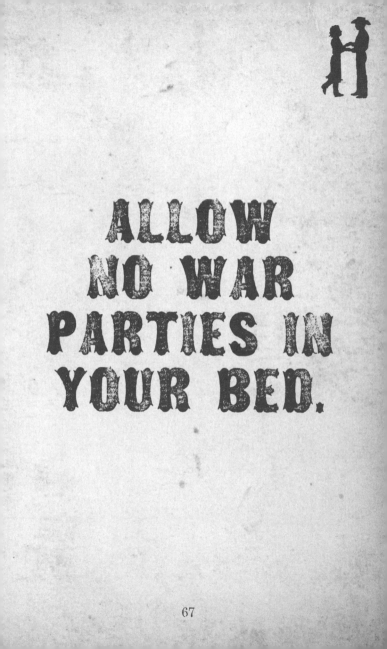

ALLOW NO WAR PARTIES IN YOUR BED.

WHEN YOU'RE
workin' a horse or
dealin' with a man,

★ ★ ★

take it slow,
take it easy,
and don't rush 'em.

There's no need for a lot of talkin' when two people understand each other.

THE SECRET TO A LONG LIFE IS TO BE WILLIN' TO GROW OLDER.

NOBODY'S CREDIT IS BETTER THAN THEIR MONEY.

If you don't
EXPECT
much,

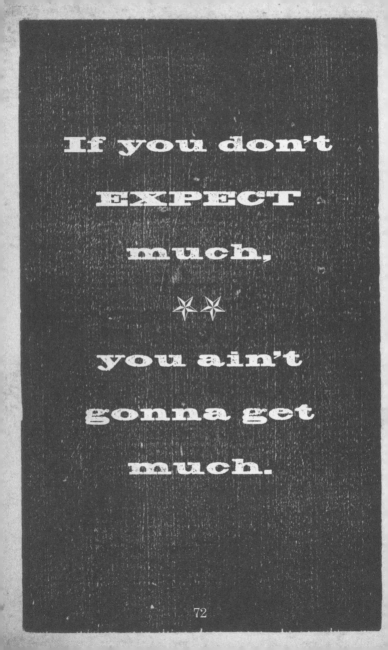

you ain't
gonna get
much.

Crack your own whip.

DON'T LET
anybody else
do it for you.

IT'S NO BIG DEAL
cleaning house, cooking
meals, or doing laundry.
More men oughta try it.

DON'T FIND FAULT, FIND A REMEDY.

About half your troubles come
from wanting your way;

★ ★ ★

the other half come from
GETTIN' IT.

**Opportunity
may knock
just once, but
temptation is a
frequent visitor.**

THE MORE
INCHES YOU
GIVE A MAN,
THE MORE HE
BECOMES A
RULER.

A CLEAR
conscience
is a restful
pillow.

A weddin' ring
should cut off
the wearer's
circulation.

If you build walls
around yourself,
don't be surprised if it gets
kinda lonely in there.

THERE'S NO
FUTURE IN
LIVIN' IN
THE PAST.

If you get all wrapped up in yourself, you'll find you make a pretty small package.

IT'S TOUGH TO WALK AWAY
from something you love,

★ ★ ★

but sometimes it's
the only way.

DON'T TRY SO HARD
to make your man a good
husband that you don't have
time to be a good wife.

There is
a charm
about a man
who is wild.

✷✷

DON'T
FALL
FOR IT.

BE SURE THE GOIN' UP IS WORTH THE COMIN' DOWN.

Sometimes, you just need to TAKE THE BRIDLE OFF, throw the skillet away, and let the panther scream.

Don't be afraid to ride
a horse of a different color.

★ ★ ★

Sometimes it's a nice
change of pace.

Even if it takes more than one throw to land a steer and tie him, he's still roped and tied.

Gettin' up
a lynch
party
IS NOT
GROUP
THERAPY.

NEVER
SHOW
YOUR
ROLL.

IT'S EASIER TO STAY WELL THAN TO GET WELL.

Nature

TEACHES,

she never

preaches.

You can't know
everything;
★★★
neither can
ANYBODY ELSE.

Most everything you hear about a cowboy is true. But the important thing is—they take care of the cows.

Charity is not a luxury to
be acquired along the way.
IT MUST BE NURTURED
from the heart's beginning.

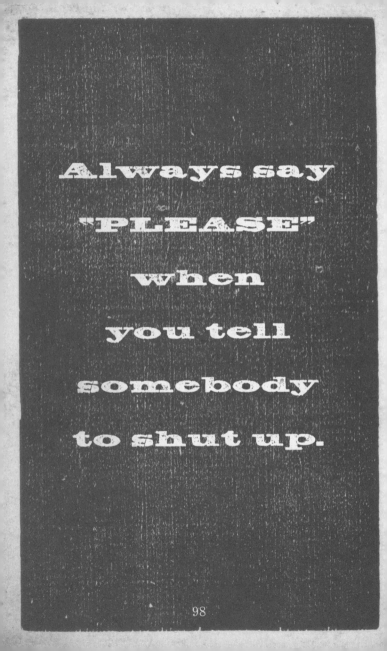

Always say
"PLEASE"
when
you tell
somebody
to shut up.

FOLKS WHO HAVE NO VICES HAVE VERY FEW VIRTUES.

When there's a drought
everybody is dry. When it
rains, everybody gets wet.
Mother Nature makes
NO DISTINCTIONS.

MOST HARD-BOILED PEOPLE ARE HALF-BAKED.

Never let
yourself be
drawn into a
game where you
do not know
the rules—
ALL the rules.

PREMATURE ULTIMATUMS
generally result from
immature considerations.

NEVER ASK A MAN THE SIZE OF HIS SPREAD!

It's not a miracle if you find an orange under an apple tree; something ain't right.

To win, all you gotta do IS GET UP one more time than you fall.

SOMETIMES IT'S SMART TO ASK A MAN'S ADVICE,

✦✦

BUT TAKIN' IT IS ANOTHER MATTER.

Everything is better shared.

Don't let anybody's opinion
kill your belief
IN YOURSELF.

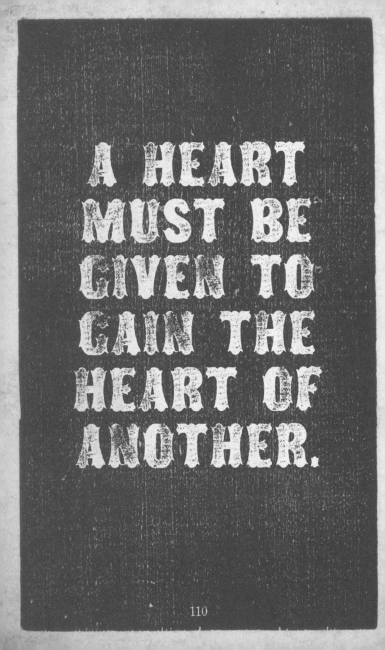

A HEART MUST BE GIVEN TO GAIN THE HEART OF ANOTHER.

WHEN YOU DISAGREE, TRY NOT TO BE DISAGREEABLE ABOUT IT.

A promise
made is a
PROMISE
KEPT.

That's how
it is on the
cowgirl
trail.

A lot of what a man knows, a woman knows better.

SPRING CALVING HELPS YOU FORGET A HARD WINTER.

Don't be afraid to
GIVE UP ON A GOOD IDEA
if the facts don't bear it out.

Before you get serious
with a cowboy, make sure
HE VALUES YOU
more than his truck.

Virtue is its own punishment.

Whenever you go away,
★ ★ ★
ALWAYS COME BACK
before they learn
to get on without you.

DO NOT SQUANDER YOUR PITY OR YOUR STRENGTHS.

A man who wears spurs
has high expectations.

★ ★ ★

A woman who wears spurs
has a mind of her own.

Just because a man says it's so, don't mean IT IS.

RIDE the high country,
see through God's eyes.
RIDE the desert,
feel God's strength.
RIDE the prairies,
hear God's voice.

STARRY NIGHTS QUIET THE SOUL.

If you're fixin'
to get yourself
a good stallion,
don't go lookin'
in the donkey
corral.

Never venture onto THIN ICE with a fancy skater.

Avoid any food that would gag a BUZZARD.

EVEN A FOOL
CAN BE RIGHT
SOME OF THE
TIME.

IT'S RŌDEO, NOT RODÉO.

A HORSE IS CONSIDERED
well trained when he is
convinced that he wants to do
what you want him to do.

Convincing
yourself
that a bad
idea is a
good one,
IS A BAD
IDEA.

Keep plenty of good hay in
the barn and you'll find it's a
fact that a smart horse never
FORGETS THE WAY HOME.

FROM TIME
TO TIME, FIND
YOURSELF
A PLACE SO
PEACEFUL
THAT YOU CAN
ENTER THE
QUIET.

Recognizing
simple
certainties can
sometimes
lead to the
wildest ideas.

GIVEN A CHOICE
BETWEEN
SHOW AND
TELL, SILENCE
IS GOLDEN.

ONCE YOU KNOW
where you're goin', just
climb in the saddle and stay
on the trail 'til you get there.

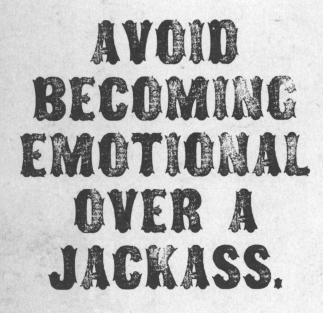

AVOID
BECOMING
EMOTIONAL
OVER A
JACKASS.

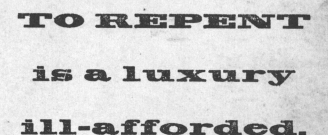

Leisure
TO REPENT
is a luxury
ill-afforded.

A good mind
moves with the
passage of time.

THERE IS A BIG
DIFFERENCE
BETWEEN A
PICNIC AND A
PILGRIMAGE.

A HARVEST TAKEN TOO EARLY WILL GIVE YOU A THIN CROP.

HORSES ALWAYS START,
they never run out of gas, and
they will not get you greasy.

Men—
You can't
live with 'em
and you can't
shoot 'em.

Baloney is baloney no matter HOW THIN you slice it.

If a man thinks that a
woman who can dog steers,
ride broncs, and rope the wind
IS TOO MUCH FOR HIM,
he's probably right.